The Matthew Journey

A Discipleship Training Manual
Through the Gospel of Matthew

by Jeff Kennedy

The Matthew Journey

A Discipleship Manual Through Matthew's Gospel

Jeff Kennedy / EssentiaLife Resources / Release Date June, 2010

essentialifepress.com
Eastpoint Church Discipleship Resources:
The EssentiaLife Curriculum Series
15303 E. Sprague Ave
Spokane Valley, WA 99037

ISBN-10:0615579027
ISBN-13:978-0615579023

Table of Contents

Introduction

"The greatest issue facing the world today, with all its heartbreaking needs, is whether those who, by profession or culture, are identified as 'Christians' will become disciples – students, apprentices, practitioners – of Jesus Christ, steadily learning from him how to live the life of the Kingdom of the Heavens into every corner of human existence."
Dallas Willard

---

*I*f I can get away with it, I will purchase a scratch and dent display item from the store rather than a box full of "do it yourself" parts. Why? Because the thought of spending hours with tedious instructions and assembling hundreds of pieces of a mini kitchen set is NOT my idea of a fun time. Just opening the box and surveying all the complimentary glues and wrenches from the manufacturer is enough to send me into anaphylactic shock!

My wife learned this about me the first week we were married. I purchased an entertainment center from a large national conglomerate. I brought the item home, tore open the box and proceeded to assemble the unit in record time. When the dust cleared, I had lost my religion and my wife's respect for me.

With the finished but shifty entertainment center completed, I proudly showed my wife the bag of screws and pieces left over from the project. My wife saw the bag of proprietary bolts and blurted out, "Aren't these supposed to be *in the entertainment* center?" To which I answered, "No Dear! The manufacturer always supplies extra bolts, just in case you loose a few." She replied (fighting the urge to laugh) "So, the manufacturer thinks you are going to lose *40 bolts?*"

You see, the problem is that I never once looked at the instructions. Whether it's a car, a bike, or an entertainment center, I have always struggled with having the patience to work through an instruction manual on things. But through the years I have learned that there are certain endeavors where following instructions simply cannot be avoided! Elton Trueblood once said, "Holy shoddy is still shoddy." In a similar way as believers, if we fail to follow the Master's teaching and his way, we will end up with a rickety and flimsy Christian life.

And many disciples of Jesus do just that. The trend of our modern reformed Christianity is to land much weight on teaching the doctrine of grace and to ignore the many scriptural directives for how to live the Spirit filled life. Afraid that we will somehow slip into a soft legalism, we can run the risk of neglecting some of the most important commands that Jesus gave his disciples.

Welcome to *The Matthew Journey!* Over the next 13 weeks, we will explore the discipleship content found in the Gospel of Matthew. Despite my past with "manual trauma," I have discovered that Matthew's Gospel is a powerful tool for life transformation. It is my sincere hope that over the next 13 weeks you will discover the life-changing power of God's Word. It is truly a joy to tap such a rich resource for life development.

Matthew's Tall Order

Before Jesus left his disciples he gave them the famous commission to "Go, therefore, and make disciples of all nations, baptizing them in the name of the Father, and of the Son, and of the Holy Spirit, and **teaching them to obey everything that I've commanded you**..." (Mt 28:19-20). The commission actually reveals a unique characteristic of Matthew's Gospel - *it was designed to be a training manual for the Matthean* *community of disciples.*[1]

Matthew's Gospel was structured along five major discourses on discipleship (Ch's 5-7; 10; 13; 18; 24-25). In addition to these formalized sermons, the gospel contains numerous situational teaching moments. Thus, future disciples are expected to assimilate the entire spectrum of Jesus' teaching content found in both His preaching and practice.[2] The disciple of Jesus should know:

- who Jesus *is*
- what Jesus has to *say*, and
- what Jesus *did*.

Knowing who he is will inspire *faith* in him. Knowing what he commands will guide the disciple in obedience, and knowing what the Master does will provide a pattern to follow. These three lines of inquiry will guide the disciple's development into the image of Jesus. The end game in following such a manual is that the believer will be prepared to make disciples of others.

If this all sounds to you like a pretty tall order, well then you're right. It is a demanding journey! This is why several core convictions will guide this discipleship course. Let's look briefly at these beliefs.

Core Convictions About Discipleship

First, discipleship begins at the cross. I recently read a book by a famous author who stated very clearly that, "All disciples are believers, but not all believers are disciples." However from a biblical perspective, this idea of a hierarchy of belief is simply wrong. In the Scriptures, we see that disciples *are* believers who have experienced the

---

1 Michael Wilkins, "Matthew" in *The NIV Application Commentary* (Grand Rapids: Zondervan, 2004), 21. See the discussion of *entellomai* (to command).

2 Samuel Byrskog, *Jesus the Only Teacher: Didactic Authority and Transmission in Ancient Israel, Ancient Judaism, and the Matthean Community* (Almqvist & Wiksell International: Stockholm, 1994), 321. Byrskog documents that the ancients practiced a "hearing and doing hermeneutic" based on the rhetoric and lifestyle of the Master.

transforming power of God's grace and mercy.[3] Any attempt to form a rigid dichotomy between "believers" and "real disciples" is a forced distinction and *not* a biblical *one*. Embracing the scandal of Jesus' cross is both the entry point and describes the ongoing lifestyle of self-denial that should characterize every believer.

Secondly, life transformation is a Spirit-empowered enterprise.[4] As a believer in Jesus, we are empowered by the Spirit to live a godly life (Rom 6:1-8:11). To attempt to live and embody all that Christ commands, both in word and deed, would be impossible without what Gordon Fee calls, "God's Empowering Presence."[5] When

Why Matthew?

This discipleship mentoring approach focusses on the Gospel of Matthew instead of a more topical study of discipleship for several reasons.

1. It assists the disciple in mastering one book of the Bible. There are many fine topical manuals of discipleship on the market today that cover everything from mentoring to leadership development. But, the distinctive feature of *The Matthew Journey* is that it focusses on the discipleship material in Matthew's Gospel with a view to studying the rest of the New Testament (and the Old). When the disciple completes the material, he will have attained a sure footing in both the Old and New Testaments. Which leads us to the second reason for the Matthew study.

2. Matthew's Gospel is a critical link between Old and New Testaments. Matthew is both a portal to the past and a window into the rest of the New Testament. No other Gospel captures Jesus' fulfillment of prophecies and promises the way Matthew does. At the same time, Matthew also introduces nearly every major Christian doctrine found in the New Testament. For example, we may be tempted to think that Paul owns the patent on the doctrine of "grace." But, Matthew's Gospel is filled with Jesus' scandalous acts of grace for the crowds.* So, this critical New Testament doctrine of grace is grounded in the actions and teachings of Jesus the Messiah, which leads us to the third reason for focussing on Matthew.

3. Matthew's Gospel is a discipleship training manual. Though scholars sometimes quibble about the purpose of Matthew, the reader is inexorably led to Jesus' statement, "Go and make disciples...teaching them to obey all that I've commanded you" (Mt 28:20). First century disciples were expected to assimilate the full spectrum of their master's teaching. This teaching included both verbal exposition and the example of the master. Matthew's Gospel is arranged along five major discourses all ending with the same phrase, "when he had finished saying these things." Moreover, the sermons have a direct application to the narratives that follow them. So, Jesus teaches the disciples in both word and deed. This inherent "training-orientation" of Matthew naturally lends itself to our study.

3 Michael Wilkins, *Following the Master: A Biblical Theology of Discipleship* (Grand Rapdis: Zondervan, 1992), 257. Wilkins points out that there is no hierarchical system in the Scriptures, especially when one takes into account the way Luke used the Greek terms *mathetai* (disciples) and *pistoi* (believers).

4 Michael Wilkins, *In His Image: Reflecting Christ in Everyday Life* (Colorado Springs: NavPress, 1997), 89.

5 Gordon Fee, *God's Empowering Presence* (Peabody Massachusetts: Hendrickson Publishers, 1992).

believers are saved and regenerated by the Spirit, they are empowered to bear the fruit of righteousness (Gal 5:22) and to proclaim Jesus to their community (Acts 1:8).

Thirdly, spiritual growth isn't automatic. In order to be formed into the image of Jesus' we need God's authoritative voice – the Scriptures! Without the careful application of the Scriptures (Eph 5:15), the man/woman of God cannot possibly become all that Jesus intends for them to be. Though the Spirit gives each of us the raw material and the motivation to change, this change will never take place without an active participation on the part of the believer.[6] We are transformed by the renewing of our minds (Rom 12:1-2) and the application of Jesus' teaching to our lives (Mt 7:24-26).

Fourthly, discipleship is actualized in community. The format for this particular course is a "micro group" of 3 to 4 people.[7] However, the material is certainly not limited to this size group. Whatever format is chosen, it is vital that the disciple actively engages the community of faith. The many allusions to community in the New Testament are not merely *descriptive*, they are *prescriptive*. Though we observe in the Bible that disciples grow in a variety of venues (small, medium, and large gatherings), believers cannot reach their full potential without the critical process of peer evaluation and encouragement. A small group format is ideal for this type of course.

And lastly, discipleship is a lifelong process.[8] The disciple should avoid the expectation that after he completes a course, a small group, or a discipleship program, that he will then be the "total package" for Christ. Even the Apostle Paul stated that he would "press on" and take new ground in his journey toward ultimate resurrection (Phil 3:10-12).

---

6 Dallas Willard, *Renovation of the Heart: Putting on the Character of Christ* (Colorado Springs: NavPress, 2002), 95-96.

7 Greg Ogden, *Transforming Discipleship* (Downers Grove: IVP, 2003), 15.

8 Wilkins, *In His Image*, 61.

* Though the Gospels were likely composed after Paul's epistles, we should keep in mind that the Jesus stories had been in circulation for decades prior to the composition of the letters of Paul. Thus, when Paul quotes the Jesus sayings, he is drawing from the same Gospel traditions that Matthew and the rest of the Gospel authors had access to.

Overview of the Journey

So, here's how to proceed. Before week one, each participant will need to read through Matthew's Gospel from beginning to end, at least once. Session one provides an overview of the journey, an orientation to the approach, and a glossary of terms.

Here is a sample of the major sections in each of the weekly sessions to be discussed as time allows.

Overview of the Journey Week 1

How To Use This Study Guide

Engaging the Text

Engaging the Biblical texts. This step is critical as we explore the *content* of Scripture. Read the passages deeply.

Exploring the Context

Becoming familiar with the big picture. This next step involves going beyond the immediate content to examining the *flanking contexts* of the primary passages, the *lateral contexts* found in other Gospels, and the *theological contexts* articulated in the epistles and elsewhere.

Broadening Your Perspective

Broadening your perspective. Next, the disciple will explore both the inherited culture and the immediate culture of the 1st century in order to discover what bearing these details have on the text.

Journaling for Practical Application

Journaling your observations. Finally, the disciple will interpret and apply the passage to his own life. Devotional reflection is the last step in this process.

Commit to praying for fellow disciples in the group.

Preparation for Week One

1. Read Matthew's Gospel from beginning to end, at least once.
2. Be sure to note often repeated emphases and themes. What does Matthew assert to be true about Jesus? How does Jesus react to the crowd verses the religious authorities? Note Jesus' relation to the OT (Old Testament).
3. Be prepared to discuss your observations and initial impressions of Matthew in week one.
4. Prayerfully consider growth opportunities in your own discipleship as you read through the Gospel. Write them down and be prepared to discuss them in session one.
5. Pray for the other participants in your group.

Glossary of Terms

Yahweh: This is the Old Testament name that God gave himself to Moses. It is most often translated with all caps as "LORD."

Theology: The word "theology" comes from two Greek terms: *theos*, meaning "God" and *logia*, meaning "the study of." Theology is the study of God.

Eschatology: The word "eschatology" is a compound of two Greek terms: *eschatos*, meaning "last things" and *logia*, meaning "the study of." Eschatology is that branch of theology (see below) that is concerned with the study of the end times or last things.

Apocalyptic: This word comes from the Greek term *apocalupsis*, meaning "to reveal, or unveil." "Apocalyptic" deals with the revelation of certain mysteries and is a formal genre (type of literature e.g. Revelation, Ezekiel, Daniel etc.) that was prominent from 200 BC to 200 AD.

Messiah: The word "messiah" is a transliteration (sounds the same) as the Hebrew word *Messhiach*, and means "the anointed one." It refers to the King who would rule in an everlasting dynasty coming from the line of David (hence the term *Davidic Messiah*).

2nd Temple Judaism: This was the second temple built by the Jews after their return from exile in Babylonia (519 BC). Cyrus the Great allowed Jews to return and rebuild their city. In 19 BC, Herod the Great undertook a massive renovation of the temple. This temple was destroyed in 70 AD, ending the period called "2nd Temple Judaism" and marking the beginning of "Tannaitic Judaism."

Son of Man: Is an apocalyptic term (see above on *apocalyptic*) referring to the Messiah as the Supreme and glorified ruler (see Dan. 7). This term also can be used to say "I" or "I myself" in some contexts.

Rabbi: The hebrew term *ravi* (*rabbi*) *means* "master of me." It was a general term of respect for a wise teacher or sage during the 2nd temple period. However, after the destruction of the temple this term came to designate a trained scholar of Judaism who had studied to become an ordained Jewish cleric.

Disciple: This word generally refers to any follower of an established master-teacher. The term is used in the New Testament to refer to those who had moved into an exclusive and committed association with the Jesus the Master.

Synagogue: This word literally means "assembling together." A synagogue was the center of religious and community life in the ancient Jewish world. After the destruction of the temple (70 AD), the synagogue would become a local academy of learning and education.

Temple: The temple was the symbol of Jewish life and existence. The temple was the place where Yahweh dwelled, forgave the nations sins, and where many sacrifices and rituals were carried out. The temple was the place where heaven and earth intersected - it was a nexus between this life and the next.

Kingdom of Heaven: This was the Jewish view of the political and spiritual reign of the Messiah. The Kingdom of Heaven was to be established by Christ on earth, and was not viewed as something that merely existed in the afterlife somewhere. Jesus used this phrase to communicate God's rule in the hearts and lives of people, rather than a geopolitical Kingdom.

Pharisees: A very religious and pious sect of men who were well respected in Jewish culture. The term "pharisees" literally means "the separate ones." These pious rabbis distinguished themselves by mastering a dizzying compliment of purity rituals. They considered themselves holy and set apart for the special study and service of Yahweh. They attempted to sway the political landscape through religious reform. Jesus had more in common with Pharisaic theology than any other Jewish sect.

Sadducees: A materialistic religious movement that had purely political aspirations. These men along with the Pharisees, comprised the "Sanhedrin" or the ruling council of Israel. They wielded great political influence until they were destroyed in 70 AD, leaving only the Pharisees.

Herodians: This was a political party who followed Herod the King. They were compromisers with Rome and were known for choosing political expedience over religious commitment.

Torah: The first five books of the Bible (Genesis, Exodus, Leviticus, Numbers, and Deuteronomy), or also another name for the entire Old Testament. The Jews in Jesus' day read the Old Testament as their Bible, and they based their identity as a nation from the stories of Creation, Exodus from Egypt, and taking possession of the Promised Land. Additionally, most of their various national symbols such as circumcision, Sabbath, and kosher dietary laws can be found in the first five books of the Old Testament.

Matthew's Theology pt. 1 Week 2

Engaging the Text

In this first leg of the journey, we will unpack Matthew's theology. Though most of us tend to think about Christian doctrine from a Pauline perspective, Matthew introduces the believer to nearly every foundational Christian teaching.

Look specifically at the content. Read the primary texts. What claims do they make?

Read
Matt. 1:1 "A record of the genealogy of Jesus the Messiah, the son of David, the son of Abraham."

Matthew's Christology
1. The Son of God: Begin by reading Chapters 1 and 2 of Matthew; see also 3:17; 14:33; 17:5; 26:63. How is the term "Son of God" used by Matthew as it applies to Jesus?

2. The Son of David: Next, read 1:1; 9:27; 12:23; 15:22; 20:30; and 21:9-15. How is the phrase, "Son of David" used the same or differently in these passages?

3. The Christ (Messiah): Read 1:18; 11:2; 16:16-20; 22:42; 23:10; 24:5, 23; 26:63; 27:17-22. As you read these passages, how is the term "Christ" used by all these differing people, including Jesus?

4. The Lord of His Assembly (Church): Read 16:18; 18:15-20. Why do you think Matthew's Gospel is the only one to use the word "church?"

5. The One Teacher of God's People: Read 8:19; 9:11; 10:24; 12:38; 19:16; 22:16-36; 23:8-10; 26:18; 28:19-21. How do these passages present Jesus as a teacher? Looking specifically at 23:8-10, and 28:19-20 - how is Jesus' role as a teacher different than his rabbinic competitors?

6. The Son of Man:
- Read 8:20; 11:19; and 12:32-40. How does the phrase "the son of man" appear to be used in these passages?

- Next, read 16:13, 17:9-22; 20:18-28; 26:24-45. What does the title "Son of Man" refer to here?

- Now, read 10:23; 13:37-41; 19:28; 24:27-44; 25:31; 26:64. How is the title used in these passages?

Matthew's Theology

Matthew's theology plays a supporting role to his Christology (teaching about Jesus). In fact, Matthew reflects and "radicalizes" his own Jewish theology as it relates to Jesus.[9] He attempts to explain Jewish beliefs in light of Jesus the Messiah as the fulfillment of their hope. Though he does not present a systematic treatment of Christian theology, major Jewish beliefs and themes do appear episodically throughout his Gospel.

1. Jewish Monotheism: Read Mt 3:9. What do we know about the "God of Abraham?" Read 4:10. Who does Jesus say should be the ONLY object of our worship? What text is he citing?

Now read Mt 15:31. When the crowds see the miraculous power of Jesus, how do they praise God?

Next. Read Mt 16:16. How does Peter describe God in his affirmation of Jesus? How did Yahweh describe himself to Moses?

In 22:21, whom does Jesus contrast the god of the Greco-Roman world (Caesar) to?

9 John Nolland, *The Gospel of Matthew: A Commentary on the Greek Text* (Grand Rapids: Eerdmans, 2005), 38.

In 22:37, what OT passage does Jesus affirm as the most important in the Bible?

2. Grace and Mercy: Read 9:13; 12:7 (and 5:7). What does Jesus say that God values more than sacrifice? What situation was Jesus responding to when he quoted this OT passages (Hos 6:6)?

In 9:36; 14:14; 15:32, what emotion does Jesus experience when he sees the helpless crowds?

Next, read 15:22-28; 17:14-18; 18:33; 20:39-34. How does Jesus respond to people who ask him for mercy? Now, read 23:23. How does Jesus balance obedience and grace in his response to the religious leaders?

Lastly, read 8:10; 18:6; 21:25, 32. What role does faith and belief in Jesus play in Matthew's Gospel?

3. The Inspiration of the Scriptures: In 5:17, what does Jesus state that he has come to do with the Law? Abolish it or fulfill it?

In 7:12, what does Jesus say is the summation of the Law and the Prophets?

See also 22:36-38. Which commandment does Jesus say is the greatest?

4. Bodily Resurrection: Read 22:23-29. How does Jesus answer the Sadducees who denied the Pharisaic doctrine of resurrection?

Next, read 12:40-42. Who does Jesus say will "rise" at the judgment? What will they do?

In 27:62, who is concerned about Jesus' resurrection from the dead? These men feel the need to post a guard at the physical tomb. What does this say about their belief in a physical resurrection?

5. The Holy Spirit: Matthew's pneumatology (teaching about the Spirit): In 3:11, what does John say the Spirit will do when he comes?

Next, read 10:20. How is it that the Spirit of the Father will be "speaking" through the disciples when they are interrogated?

A little further in 12:22-32, Jesus states that blasphemy against the Son can be forgiven, but not blasphemy against the Spirit. To what is he referring here?

Lastly, in 28:19 Jesus states that new converts should be baptized in the name of the Father, the Son, and of the Holy Spirit. How does Matthew want us to view the Holy Spirit from passages like these?

6. Eschatology (Last Things): Read 7:21-25; and 24-25. How does Jesus portray himself with regards to the last days?

7. Jewish Particularism: Matthew's Gospel is the only one of the Synoptics (Matthew, Mark, and Luke) to articulate God's fulfillment of his promise to offer salvation to the Jews *first* (10:5; 15:24). Though Matthew maintains these authentic sayings of Jesus, he undeniably sets the stage for an implicit Gentile universalism (extending salvation to the Gentiles). Read 2:1-12; 4:15; 8:5-13; 15:21-28; 21:33-43; 22:1-10; 24:14; 28:18-20).

8. The Church: Read 16:18; 18:15-20.

9. The Trinity: In 28:19, the disciples are authorized to baptize new coverts into the "name" (singular) of the Father, of the Son, and of the Holy Spirit. Though Matthew does not give us a fully articulated Trinitarian system of belief, it is impossible to deny the prominence of this "Father, Son, Spirit" motif in the rest of Scripture. What do you make of this?

10. The Intermediate State: Read 5:22-30; 10:28; 18:9; 23:33. Jesus warned his hearers concerning "being thrown into" "being cast" and "being sentenced" to hell. Now read 5:12; 6:20; 11:23; 18:10; 19:21. All of these passage speak of "heaven" as a place the believer will "go" "inherit" and "store up treasure."

Summary

This first leg of the Matthew Journey has revealed that Jesus is the Son of God, the Messiah, and the Lord of the Church.[10] Jesus is also the One Teacher and the decisive arbiter of God's truth as revealed in the OT. Though Paul, James, and Peter provide an articulated theology through letters, Matthew chose to teach by way of narrative. Matthew's Gospel introduces us to every foundational Christian doctrine. The Gospel account teaches Christian doctrine (or realized Jewish theology) implicitly through these timeless stories.

---

10 Michael Wilkins, "Matthew," 25.

Matthew's Theology pt.2 Week 3

Engaging the Text

Immediate Contexts (this week is optional if time does not permit the participants to cross reference Matthew's teaching with the rest of the New Testament).
In the 2nd week, we were able to look at the immediate contexts of the many passages that we studied. So for this week only, we will rely on that as we look at the parallel contexts (from other Synoptic Gospels) and the broader theological contexts of the Epistles.

Lateral Contexts
1. **The Son of God:** Mark 1:1; Luke 1:35; John 3:18

2. **The Son of David:** Mark 12:35; Luke 18:38

3. **The Christ (Messiah):** Mark 8:29; Luke 9:20

4. **The Lord of His Assembly (Church):**

5. **The One Teacher of God's People:** Mark 13:1; Luke 21:7

6. The Son of Man: Mark 8:31; Mark 9:12; Mark 13:26; Mark 14:62; Luke 22:69

Theological Contexts

Let's take some time to view a cross section of Christian theology from other NT authors. As we take the time to bring Paul, Peter, John and others into Matthew's material, what similarities or possible differences do you see with these other Biblical theologians?

1. Jewish Monotheism:
Gal 3:20; 1 Cor 8:6; Eph 4:6; 1 Tim 2:5

2. Grace and Mercy:
Jn 1:14-17 ; Acts 15:11; Rom 3:20-24; Eph 2:8-10; 1 Pet 1:10-11

3. The Inspiration of the Scriptures:
2 Tim 3:16; 2 Pet 1:20-21; Jn 10:34-36; 1 Cor 14:37

4. Bodily Resurrection
Acts 23:6; Acts 24:14; Rom. 1:4; 1Cor. 15:12; Heb. 11:35; 1Pet. 1:3

5. The Holy Spirit:
Acts 1:8; Acts 5:3, 5; Titus 3:5; Gal. 3:2; Eph. 1:13

6. Eschatology (Last Things)
Acts 2:17; 1 Thes 4:15-17 15; 2Th. 2:1

7. Jewish Particularism
Rom. 1:16; 10:21

8. The Church
Eph. 1:22; 1Tim. 3:15

9. The Trinity
Gal. 4:6; Rom. 8:9; 1Cor. 2:11; 1Cor. 3:16; Heb 1:2; 1John 5:20; Titus 2:13

Broadening Your Perspective

Considering the Inherited Culture (the OT)
What bearing does the Old Testament have on these passages?
More than any other Gospel, Matthew draws on the OT to make his case regarding Jesus the Messiah. The Gospel contains 55 unambiguous quotations of the OT (nearly the same amount as the other synoptics put together), 12 of which Matthew designates as "fulfillment" texts.[11] In addition to the direct quotations, the Gospel contains numerous allusions to the OT Scripture. Likewise, the OT text appears to be the very fabric of many of the Jesus sayings.

Considering the Immediate Culture
What significance does the culture of the New Testament have on these passages?
Messianic fervor was at an all time high during second Temple Judaism.[12] Daniel had prophesied that the "ruler" of God's people would come in the 70 Weeks prophesy (Daniel 9:24-27).[13] The Jews had anticipated the coming of the Messianic King in the decades prior to Jesus, and the Galilean region was a nexus for Messianic uprisings. The fact that Messianic expectation cooled significantly in the post-temple period is evidence that the Gospel stories took place during the period that they attest.[14] Moreover, one should note the many confrontations with the Sadducean party, which became extinct after the destruction of the temple (AD 70).

Though one would expect Jesus to take his place as the next messianic revolutionary to lead a campaign against Roman oppression, Jesus utterly rejected this approach. Instead, his Kingdom would be transformational. Jesus emphasized the importance of internal righteousness, and the locus of his kingdom activity would be the human heart. The Good News of the Kingdom would not be that the Gentiles are finally getting what's coming to them. The surprising truth of King Jesus' economy was that God would now call the outsiders to become insiders by faith in the world's true Messiah.

---

11 Craig L. Blomberg, "Matthew" *Commentary on the New Testament Use of the Old*, Gen Ed. G.K. Beale and D.A. Carson (Grand Rapids: Baker Academic, 2007), 1. It must be stressed that many of the prophecies that Matthew draws on were not explicitly predictive. There are a number that are clearly and/or possibly Messianic, yet many of Matthew's "fulfillment" reflections appear to employ a typological approach.

12 Craig Keener, *The Gospel of Matthew: A Socio-Rhetorical Commentary* (Grand Rapids: Eerdmans, 2009), 61. "Second Temple Judaism" ended with the destruction of the Temple in AD 70.

13 Keener, *The Gospel of Matthew*, 61.

14 Daniel B. Wallace, *Matthew: Introduction, Argument, and Outline* (Dallas: Biblical Studies Press, 1997), 7.

Journaling for Practical Application

Consider how the passages apply to your own discipleship to Jesus.

Regarding Jesus' identity, how does Matthew intend for us to understand Him? Take some time to reflect and respond to Jesus. Record your prayers and make them very personal.

_____

_____

_____

_____

_____

_____

_____

_____

_____

_____

_____

Take a moment to reflect on your understanding of Christian doctrine. How does

believing rightly about the following effect how you live day to day?

Is Jesus the Lord and Master of your life? Why or why not?

_____

_____

_____

_____

_____

_____

_____

How is the person of the Holy Spirit empowering you for life change and mission?

_____

_____

_____

_____

_____

_____

_____

_____

_____

_____

How does your understanding of the "end" of all things affect the way you live today? How does your reflection on end-times themes make a difference in the way you approach your life?

_____

_____

_____

_____

_____

_____

_____

_____

_____

_____

_____

_____

Considering that Jesus is the Lord and builder of his Church (assembly), how does this effect your view of the church today? How does Paul's teaching on unity in the church set with you? Is there any way that you can self-correct in your view of the unity of the church?

_____

_____

_____

_____

_____

_____

_____

_____

_____

How should you think about the Trinitarian teaching in your own worship life? Do you see that there are various roles for the members of the Godhead (Father, Son, and Spirit)?

_____

_____

_____

_____

_____

_____

_____

_____

_____

_____

_____

The 5 Discourses: Discipleship Week 4

Discourse Number 1: The Sermon on the Mount

Introduction: Matthew depicts Jesus as a supreme teacher-sage by arranging his Gospel along five major discourses. The five major speeches show Jesus teaching on the mount with uncommon authority (5:1-7:29), offering practical and prophetic instruction to his disciples for their missions (10:1-42), revealing the mystery of the Kingdom through parables (13:1-53), and challenging the conventional wisdom of his day (18:1-19:2). In Jesus' final discourse, he exhorts his followers to watchfulness, faithfulness, and compassionate service while the Master is away (24:1-25:46).[15]

Read Matthew chapters 5-7: This sermon gives us a sample, or a cross section of the kind of ethical behavior that should attend the disciple's life. Its primary purpose is to establish that Jesus has the authority to be the final, decisive arbiter of truth and the judge of ones eternal status. This sermon sets the pace for numerous subsequent teaching moments in which Jesus assumes the right to speak with God's authoritative voice. He is the one true teacher of God's people (Mt 23:8, 10).

Read 5:1-2. Who does Jesus call to himself and teach? What posture does the Rabbi take when he teaches them?

15 D.A. Carson, "Matthew" in *The Expositors Bible Commentary,* F.E. Gaebelein (ed.), vol. 8 (Grand Rapids: Zondervan, 1984), 495.

The word "beatitude" in Greek is *makarioi* where we get the term *makarism*. It means literally, "blessing statement." How does Jesus use the "beatitudes" (blessing statements) at the beginning of chapter 5 to portray himself? What does Jesus say Kingdom people are like?

In 5:16, Jesus tells them that others should see their good works.

In 5:17-20, Jesus addresses the issue of the "righteousness" of the scribes and Pharisees. How is it that the disciples "good works" could possibly exceed that of the pious religious leaders (see v. 19, 20)?

In 5:21-43, why do you think Jesus begins each paragraph with the phrase, "You have heard it said..."? Where had they heard it said, and what is "it" (5:21, 27, 31, 33, 38, 43)?

As you look at each paragraph, how does Jesus address the intention of each of the laws?
- Hatred is

- Murder (5:21-26)

- Lust is Adultery (5:27-30)

- Commitment vs. Divorce (5:31-32)

- Honesty and Oaths (5:33-37)

- Rights and Retaliation (5:38-42)

- Surpassing Love (5:43-48)

Next, read 6:1-18. What pious activity does Jesus use to illustrate the difference between internal and external religion (6:2, 5, 16)?

As you read 6:19 - 7:7-11, how does Jesus address attitudes and intentions of the heart regarding:

- Investments (6:19-24)

- Worry (6:25-34)

- A Critical Spirit toward a Brother (7:1-5)

- Good Judgment with Sacred Things (7:6)

- Requests to God (7:7-11)

In 7:12, Jesus famously sums up the law in what important ancient maxim or saying? Does the emphasis of this saying appear to be on external righteousness (5:17-20), or an inward concern for others?

Next, read 7:13-27. Jesus establishes criteria for entering the Kingdom in a series of contrasts. For what reasons are people turned away from the Kingdom in the following analogies?

- 2 Doors (7:13)

- 2 Trees (7:17)

- 2 Houses (7:24)

Finally, the crowd notes that Jesus teaches with an unprecedented authority (7:28-29). How does Jesus' teaching appear to be uniquely authoritative?

The 5 Discourses: Discipleship Week 5

Engaging the Text

Discourse Number 1 cont... The Sermon on the Mount

Immediate Contexts

First, the sermon is flanked by extraordinary healings and miraculous activity. After Jesus had relocated his ministry base to Capernaum (4:13), he then set out to proclaim his Kingdom Gospel. Matthew states, "from that time on, Jesus began to preach and say, 'Repent, for the Kingdom of Heaven is at hand'" (4:17). Matthew then offers a summary of Jesus' ministry characterized by teaching in synagogues, proclaiming the gospel of his Kingdom, and healing every kind of sickness and disease among the Judeans (4:23). This is followed by Jesus' inaugural sermon (5-7) and after the teaching on the mount ends Jesus descends to continue his miraculous activity (8:1ff.). Matthew portrays Jesus as not only teaching with authority, but exceeding rabbinic authority by performing miracles at will.

Lateral Contexts

Take a few minutes and read through Luke's version of Jesus' sermon.
Luke 6:17-49

How is Luke's version of Jesus' famous Sermon on the Mount different than Matthew's?

Do you think these are the same sermons? Why or why not?

Theological Contexts

Read Romans 3:19-24. What kind of righteousness does Paul say is now revealed? How was this different from the "righteousness of the Pharisees and Scribes" that Jesus mentioned in Mt 5:20?

In Ephesians 2:8-10, Paul states that we are saved by grace through faith - *not by works*. He then states that a life of grace produces *good works* (v.10). With this in mind, how does Jesus use the phrase "good works" in Mt 5:16?

Colossians 3:13 states that we are to "forgive one another, just as the Lord has forgiven you." This saying comes directly from Mt 6:14 when Jesus states, "For if you forgive others their trespasses, your heavenly Father will forgive yours."

In 1 Cor 7:1-12, Paul appears to be quoting and amending Jesus' saying on divorce in Mt 5:31. What do you make of Paul taking this kind of liberty with the Jesus saying?

In Mt 7:21-23, Jesus makes it clear that only those who "do the will of the Father" will enter the Kingdom. He then explains this by contrasting the "many who will come" with an impressive resume of charismatic activity with those whom he "knows." John also states in 1 Jn 2:17 that "those who do the will of God will live forever."
Jesus also states that "this is eternal life, that they may know you - the one true God and Jesus the Christ whom you've sent."

Broadening Your Perspective

Considering the Inherited Culture (the OT)

How does the Old Testament factor into Jesus' Sermon?
The backdrop for Mt 5:21-48 is in Exodus 20:1-17, Moses receives the Ten Commandments. In Deut 5:1-21, Moses reiterates these commands. These commands (some vertical and some horizontal) constitute the core of Jewish theology. The "decalogue" as it is called (meaning 10 laws) also seems to be at the very heart of Jesus' own teaching.
So, do you think that Jesus is mirroring Moses on the Mountain? What similarities to the Exodus account are there?   What is dissimilar and doesn't match the giving of the Mosaic law?

Matthew uses the Greek version of the ten commandments (LXX - or "Septuagint"), and portrays Jesus as idealizing these commands. The key to Jesus' approach is the internalization of the law.

The Sermon concludes with an appeal to the "Two Ways" genre of Jewish literature.[16] This is rooted in Moses' challenge and warning found in Deut 30:1-20. It seems that Jesus is once again putting two paths before the Jewish nation. They may choose "life" or they may choose the wide road which inexorably leads to destruction.

Considering the Immediate Culture

What significance does the culture of the New Testament have on these passages?
As noted above, in many ways Jesus' teaching was very similar to that of his contemporaries. It was common for popular itinerate rabbis to be invited to speak in the synagogues (4:23) or to offer their disciples a kind of field education (5:1-7:29).[17] Additionally, it was customary for Jewish teachers to use a variety of rhetorical devices such as parables, anecdotes, hyperbole, questions, and riddles in order to communicate effectively.[18] Carson states, "Virtually all the statements in chapters 5-7 (sic) can be paralleled in the Talmud or other Jewish sources."[19] An example would be the blessing

---

16 Craig Blomberg, *Commentary on the New Testament*, 30.

17 Brad Young, *Meet the Rabbis* (Peabody: Hendrickson Publishers, 2007), 29. See also Keener, The IVP Bible Background Commentary: New Testament (Downers Grove: Intervarsity Press, 1993), 55.

18 Keener, *A Socio-Rhetorical Commentary*, 25. Keener provides a very good digest of the various kinds of Jewish sages and teachers that likely existed in Jesus' day.

19 Carson, "Matthew,"126. Though, Carson states that this is not difficult considering the sheer size of these later rabbinic documents.

(*makarios*) statements compared to 4Q525 of the Dead Sea collection,[20] and the well-established Semitic idiom, "he opened his mouth" (5:2).[21] In this way, Jesus appears in Matthew's text as a typical teacher and preacher in the region of Galilee.

Yet, Jesus' teachings were far more than midrashic expositions or cleverly worded aphorisms.[22] The impression that emerges from the Matthean sermon is of an important teacher whose authority exceeds that of his contemporary scribal Jews, the pious Pharisees, or for that matter Moses himself.

20 Craig Evans, "Matthew – Luke" in *The Bible Knowledge Background Commentary* (Colorado Springs: David C. Cook Publishers, 2005), 102. The Dead Sea Scrolls are given reference designations like "4QMMT" or "4Q525" to help scholars find their place in the literature, just as we use "John 1:1" as reference markers.

21 John Nolland, *The Gospel of Matthew*, 191.

22 Midrash here is simply referring to interpretive tendencies among rabbis and should not be pressed too far.

Journaling for Practical Application

Consider how the passages apply to your own discipleship to Jesus. Regarding Jesus' first sermon to his disciples, write out the character qualities that Jesus commends in 5:1-16.

How do you stack up? Take some time to prayerfully consider how you can move toward a life characterized by the beatitudes.

_____
_____
_____
_____
_____
_____
_____
_____
_____
_____
_____
_____
_____

Take a moment to reflect on Jesus' high view of Scripture in (5:17-18). Respond to the following:

What is your view of the Bible? Is it the _primary_, or the _sole_ guide for your faith and practice?

_____
_____
_____
_____
_____
_____

Is it okay to be a "Bible-believing" Christian without a corresponding change? How does

5:20 change or inform your perspective on this?

Reflecting on 5:21-48, which of these commands do you struggle with the most?

- *Showing Anger:*

- *Lust and Coveting:*

- *Attitudes Toward Divorce:*

- *Empty Promises (Oaths) vs. Integrity and Action:*

_____
_____
_____
_____
_____
_____
_____

- *Desire for Retribution:*

_____
_____
_____
_____
_____

- *Love for your Enemies:*

_____
_____
_____
_____
_____
_____
_____
_____
_____
_____
_____

Consider Jesus' model prayer (6:5-18).

How would you incorporate Jesus' model of prayer into your own prayer life?

_____

_____

_____

_____

_____

_____

_____

_____

_____

_____

_____

_____

_____

_____

_____

_____

Given Jesus' instructions on possessions (6:19-34), what should be our attitude toward the fleeting things of this world? What should our heart be set on? List a few ways that Jesus' teaching on possessions should specifically change the way you approach acquiring "things?"

_____

_____

_____

_____

_____

_____

_____

According to Jesus, he is the only true judge of a person's character and eternal status.

43

How should this affect the way we view others?

_____

_____

_____

_____

_____

_____

_____

_____

_____

_____

_____

_____

_____

_____

_____

_____

_____

The 5 Discourses cont... Week 6

Discourse Number 2: Missional Instructions

Introduction: Thus far, we have discovered that Jesus is the unique Son of God who has come to establish his Kingdom mission, to fulfill the Law and the Prophets, and to demonstrate his authority by wielding unprecedented power over disease, demon oppression, and illness. After establishing his ethical standards for disciples of his Kingdom (5:1-7:28), Jesus then empowers the disciples for their mission (10:1-42).[23]

Read Chapter 10: The discourse is divided into three useful sections. Jesus tells them to go to the lost sheep of Israel instead of to the Gentile communities (vv. 5-6).[24] Second, he instructs them about the nature of their ministry (vv.7-8), which is to preach that the Kingdom of Heaven is at hand, healing, raising the dead, cleansing lepers and casting out demons. The final piece of his instruction entails the disciples' reception and rejection by the "lost sheep of Israel" (vv.11-39), and the character that should attend their mission in the face of such opposition.[25]

Read 10:1-4. Why do you think Matthew gives the names of the disciples in this passage?

---

23 Michael Wilkins, "Matthew," 384.

24 R.T. France, The Gospel of Matthew, 377.

25 Wilkins, "Matthew," 384.

Read 10:7-8. How does Jesus equip the disciples for this short term mission trip through the Galilean region?

Given that Jesus has already ministered openly to Gentiles (ch. 4:12-17), and that he ultimately commissions the disciples to reach out to the nations, why do you think Jesus tells them to go "first" to the Jews in this short trip?

In 10:15, we see that Jesus raises the issue of judgment. Cities, nations, and people groups who have rejected Jesus will someday be judged "on the day of judgment." To what do you think Jesus is referring here?

Is it ever appropriate for us to claim that Jesus will judge a nation for their rejection of his Messianic claims?

Read 10:16-25. Jesus appears to be speaking prophetically about their future missions. What should the disciples expect as they go into Caesar's world announcing that his kingdom is a sham?

In 10:26-42, what are some character traits that the disciples will need to exhibit while on this dangerous mission?

Summary: This short-term training mission is both educational and eschatological. Jesus is intent on training the disciples for future mission, but also offers the Gospel first to the Jews. He predicts that the very ones who are offered this message will reject it and reject his messengers of the new Messianic movement. The result of this rejection will be their denial before the Father, and Jesus warns the disciples to put this Kingdom mission above all other allegiances, otherwise they also would be in danger of loosing their lives (vv. 37-39).

Exploring the Context

Immediate Contexts
Chapter 10 identifies Jesus' disciples as "the Twelve Disciples." This is the point at which Matthew's Gospel turns specific attention to these individuals and their subsequent training. Jesus has inaugurated his Kingdom (ch's 1-4), articulated the standards for Kingdom life (ch's 5-7), authenticated his Messianic claims through miraculous exploits (ch's 8-9) and now has authorized his disciples to carry out his mission in the Power of the Spirit (ch 10). The subsequent chapters will show an increasing escalation with the pious Jews culminating in his crucifixion and resurrection.

Lateral Contexts
Read Mark 6:1-13. Mark's account of Jesus' rejection and instruction to his disciples is very brief. Does this passage add anything to your understanding?

In Luke 9:37-43 (see also Mt 17:14-21), the disciples appear not to have any power to heal a demon possessed boy. Where did their power go?

Theological Contexts

Read Romans 1:16. Who does Paul state the Gospel is the power of God unto salvation for *first*?

Read a little further, and who does Paul state the judgment of God will be dispensed to *first*?
How is this theme echoed in Mt 10?

Read Acts 7:52, and 9:4. In ch. 7, Stephen asks "was their ever a prophet that your ancestors didn't persecute?" And in 9:4 Jesus asks Paul, "why do you persecute me?" It seems that Jesus' prediction to the disciples came true.

Broadening Your Perspective

Considering the Inherited Culture (the OT)
How does the Old Testament factor into Jesus' Missional Instructions?

Nearly all commentators agree that the significance of Jesus choosing "twelve" is their ultimate role as leaders of the twelve tribes of Israel (19:28). The symbolism is unmistakable. Jesus is reconstituting Israel in the ministry and leadership of the twelve.[26]

Jesus teaches them that he had not "come" to bring political peace (at least initially), but instead he had "come" to bring strife and division to the earth. This statement about division among households and families in vv. 34-36 comes from Micah 7:6 which states, "For son treats father contemptuously, daughter rises up against her mother, daughter-in-law against her mother-in-law; A man's enemies are the men of his own household."

Considering the Immediate Culture
What significance does the culture of the New Testament have on these passages?

It is likely that Jesus was aware of the traditional interpretation of Micah 7:6, which as Keener notes "applied the familial division of this text to the period of messianic woes, the great tribulation that would precede the Messiah's coming (m. Sota. 9:15; Pesiq. Rab Kah. 5:9; Song Rb. 2.13, 4, Pesiq R. 15:14,15)."[27] For all involved (both preacher and recipients) it is reception of Jesus as Messiah that will be the deciding factor in the final analysis of ones life.[28]

---

26 Craig Blomberg, *Commentary on the New Testament*, 35.

27 Keener, *A Socio-Rhetorical Commentary*, 330. Keener goes on to note that "Jewish writers associated familial division with the final tribulation without explicitly referring to the Micah prophecy" (Jub. 23.16, 19; cf. 1 Enoch 56:7; Gk. Ezra 3:12-13; 2 Tim 3:2)."

28 R.T. France, *The Gospel of Matthew*, 184; 408. France does not see a necessary preexistent theology in Matthew, but views this as more significant as a statement of mission (9:13; 20:28; 10:34-35). However, Carson views these "I have come" statements as clear Christological and eschatological self-awareness statements of Jesus, 257.

Journaling for Practical Application

Reflect on those in your life who need the message of Jesus, and the power of the Spirit to set them free from: addiction, self-indulgence and self-centeredness, deception, and physical suffering. How might Jesus commission you to be a light of faith and faithfulness in their lives?

Write their names down followed by a simple strategic prayer.

_____

_____

_____

_____

_____

_____

_____

_____

_____

_____

Take a moment to reflect on times when you've been persecuted for your faith:

How did you respond? What would you have said or done differently? Record one recent instance.

_____

_____

_____

_____

_____

_____

_____

_____

_____

_____

How might Jesus give you his "words" to say when you are confronted by challenges from unbelievers? How would this work practically for you? Do you think this means you shouldn't be prepared ahead of time for those challenges?

_____

_____

_____

_____

_____

_____

_____

_____

_____

_____

Given Jesus' instructions at the end of chapter 10, how might you stand firm and protect your faith, your heart, and your mind when insulted and attacked by unbelievers?[29]

_____

_____

_____

_____

_____

_____

_____

29 Michael Wilkins, "Matthew," 408.

The 5 Discourses cont...   Week 7

Engaging the Text

Discourse Number 3: The Secret Kingdom

Introduction: The third discourse begins with large crowds surrounding Jesus at the shore. Once again, he takes the posture of a teacher by sitting, and instead of a hillside, he uses a boat as his platform. Jesus instructs his followers and the crowds using a series of parables to reveal something about the Kingdom that was quite unexpected.

Read Chapter 13:1-53: A curious feature of this third discourse is that the disciples want to know why he speaks to the crowd in parables. Jesus responds that this was in fulfillment of the prophet Isaiah (Is 6:9) that the Jews would ever be hearing and seeing but never comprehending despite the overexposure of Torah study and the general climate of Messianic fervor (13:13-15). He tells the disciples, "to you it has been granted to know the mysteries of the Kingdom of Heaven, but to them it has not been granted" (13:11).[30] Jesus speaks to the crowd cryptically (13:1-3) but the explanation is for insiders (10-23; 36-43).[31]

In the parable of the sower, Jesus contrasts good soil with various types of poor soil. In the parables of the weeds (13:24-30) and the net (13:47-50), there is a separation between the wheat and weeds (at harvest time) and the good fish and the bad. In the parable of the treasure and the pearl (44-46), the emphasis is on those who realize the inestimable worth of the Kingdom, as opposed to those who do not recognize its purpose or value.

---

30 R.T. France, *The Gospel of Matthew*, 510. France views the Greek term *musterion*, as a "secret" and sees a link between Matthew's usage and Dan. 2. The "secrets" that were revealed to Daniel are not mysteries in the sense that with good detective work, one might uncover what they conceal. Instead, these mysteries are "secrets" that cannot be understood without divine revelation. Indeed, this is a favorite term of Paul and does refer in his writings to special revelation.

31 Witherington, "Matthew," *Smyth and Helwys Biblical Commentary*, 257-258. Rome responded to these kinds of messianic uprisings with the iron hand of suppression. Therefore, a premature coronation by the eager crowds would likely stunt the longevity of his Kingdom ministry and probably "short-circuit" his messianic mission. Jesus appears to be telling only his closest followers the meaning of the parables and they will be expected later to take what was whispered and shout it from the rooftops (cf. ch 10).

Question: What do all these "Kingdom" parables have in common? What is the point of comparison in all of them?

Now back up and read the beginning of the section again (13:1-17). To whom does Jesus teach the parables (v. 2)?

But, who comes in private for the understanding (vv. 10-11)?

How does this set the disciples apart from the crowd?

Summary

The unmistakable inference of this discourse is that Jesus is the King of this Kingdom, for he alone knows its secrets and reveals its mysteries to the crowd and his disciples. The parables also demonstrate that the disciples are in fact the good soil, the true wheat, the unspoiled fish, and the savvy merchants who have discovered the inestimable worth of the new Messianic Kingdom.

Exploring the Context

Immediate Contexts

Chapter 13 is a "test of responsiveness."[32] Jesus was an equal opportunity Messiah. The crowds and the religious hierarchy of Judaism had ample opportunity to follow him and to believe his message. Though he has experienced direct opposition from the religious teachers, Jesus now turns his attention to the crowds.[33] Will they hear and perceive? Will they listen and understand? From this point on, Jesus turns his attention to the Gentiles and makes fewer and fewer explicit overtures to his own people.[34]

Lateral Contexts

Read Mk 4:1-9; Lk 8:1-8. Notice how Matthew and Mark depict this scene differently. Mark quotes some different parables, as well does Luke. What does this tell you about Matthew's arrangement of the teaching material here?

Luke's Mustard Seed parable is in chapter 13 of his Gospel, but not connected to the sower parable. What does this tell you about how Gospel authors shaped these stories to teach their audiences to obey Jesus' words?

Why do you think Matthew has some content that other Gospel writers don't include?

---

32 Wilkins, "Matthew," 472.

33 Wilkins, "Matthew," 472.

34 Craig Blomberg, *Commentary on the New Testament*, 48.

Theological Contexts

In 2 Sam 7:16, the prophet states, "Your house and your Kingdom will stand before me permanently. Your dynasty will be permanent."

Dan 7:27 states that God's Kingdom will be an eternal one that will someday supplant all of the Kingdoms of the earth. This will be done without the aid or effort of human armies.

How does Jesus' Kingdom fit the bill here? How could the messiah fulfill both of these promises?

Read I Cor 15:24. What does it say that Jesus will do to the Kingdom's of the earth someday?

Rev 5:10 seems to indicate that the people of God are the Kingdom and are priests. What do you make of this language?

Broadening Your Perspective

Considering the Inherited Culture (the OT)

How does the Old Testament factor into Jesus' Kingdom Teaching?

It seems that the OT is the very fabric of Jesus' teaching and thoughts. When he is not quoting the OT directly, Jesus is often alluding to it. He stitches together a patchwork of quotes and references that comprise the core of his teachings. The parable of the sower echoes Is 55:10-11. He quotes Is 6:9-10 when asked why he teaches in parables. He then seems to cite Dan 4:12 in reference to the "birds" of the air nesting in the branches of the tree that has sprouted from a small mustard seed. Lastly, we note that Jesus is fulfilling Ps 78:2-4 in speaking to the people in parables, riddles, aphorisms, proverbs, fables and allegories.[35]

Considering the Immediate Culture

What significance does the culture of the New Testament have on this passage?

Jesus is so well known for his use of parables that one may be tempted to imagine that he invented the genre. Though Jesus certainly perfected story telling and has subsequently left us with the most memorable analogies and anecdotes of history, nevertheless Jesus inherited the tradition.[36] It is clear that Jesus' story telling is distinctly Jewish. The closest resemblance to Jesus' style of teaching would be the rabbinic Jews.[37] Though the literature of the rabbis is much later than the period it attests, the many similarities between Jesus' parables and the parables of rabbinic literature show that Jesus' story telling style is authentically Jewish. This is important because this hebraic teaching style is not what we would expect if the sayings had been invented in later centuries and merely attributed to Jesus. Especially considering the antipathy between Judaism and Christianity in the second and third centuries.

---

35 Craig Blomberg, *Commentary on the New Testament*, 50.

36 Keener, *A Socio-Rhetorical Commentary*, 372.

37 Keener, *A Socio-Rhetorical Commentary*, 372. Keener notes that story parables are largely a Jewish phenomenon in the ancient world. These type of parable appear in the prophets, intertestamental apocalyptic lit. e.g. 1 Enoch 1:2-3; 37-71 etc.

Journaling for Practical Application

Reflect on the parables and their meaning for you as a disciple of Jesus.

What kind of follower is a "Kingdom" disciple?

_____

_____

_____

_____

_____

_____

_____

_____

_____

_____

_____

_____

_____

_____

Take a moment to think about the condition of your heart.

Would you say that you're heart is hard (impenetrable) soil; good, but "rocky" (cluttered with too many allegiances) soil; receptive but "thorny" (or preoccupied) soil; or good ground that produces the Kingdom's crop?

_____

_____

_____

_____

_____

_____

_____

_____

Jesus made it clear that only the disciples who seek to understand will last (13:18-23). How do you stack up here? Does your heart long to understand Jesus' teaching?

_____

_____

_____

_____

_____

_____

In 13:44-46, Jesus repeats one of his usual themes: the cost of the Kingdom. The disciples recognize it's value and pay the cost to "buy the field." What are some costs that you've experienced in embracing Jesus' cross and his way?

_____

_____

_____

_____

_____

_____

_____

_____

_____

_____

_____

_____

_____

_____

The 5 Discourses cont... Week 8

Engaging the Text

Discourse Number 4: Community Rules - Unconventional Principles for Kingdom Life

Introduction: The fourth sermon of Jesus to the disciples is regarding a prescription for community life in the Kingdom.[38] In each section of the fourth discourse, Jesus challenged conventional wisdom. In response to a question put to him by the disciples about who is the greatest in the Kingdom of Heaven (18:1-2), Jesus called a little child to him and challenged the disciples to think of greatness in terms of humility "like this child" (v. 4). This living illustration becomes the controlling metaphor for community relations in the Kingdom.

Read Chapter 18:

In Jesus' view, how serious is it to corrupt the faith of a child intentionally (vv. 7-9)?

Who do you think the "little child" is a reference to in Jesus' analogy? Could Jesus be referring to the "little ones" (that is, the disciples) in his care? How so?

---

38 Wilkins, "Matthew" 611.

Why do you think humility is the true measure of greatness?

What should be the attitude of the church toward disciples who stumble through sin and deception? How should we restore them according to this fourth discourse (15-17)?

It seems that Peter was prematurely trying to flex his spiritual muscles when he volunteered to forgive a brother up to 7 times. However, Jesus responds to his braggadocio with a relational proposition. What should our stance be toward those who sin against us personally?

In v. 35, Jesus makes it clear that God will treat the forgiven harshly if they do not extend that forgiveness to others. What do you make of this apparent threat?

How does it seem that Jesus is tying himself to these "end times" realities such as final judgment in the afterlife?

Summary

Not only did the fourth discourse quell a simmering animosity and competitiveness that Jesus sensed among his followers, it also spelled out the ramifications of a careless disciple who is averse to forgiving his brother. The parable reminded them of the realities of God's final judgment. Community life in the Kingdom of God is marked by a greatness-through-humility approach, a careful life that doesn't cause others to stumble, and reconciled relationships.[39]

---

39 Wilkins, "Matthew," 627-629.

Exploring the Context

Immediate Contexts

Peter and several others have just come down from a mount where Jesus has revealed himself - transfigured into his heavenly glory right before their very eyes. As the glorified Messiah, Jesus confers with two noted OT figures: Moses and Elijah. Naturally, the disciples assume that he is close to revealing himself to all Jerusalem and the world this way. That of course is their hope. But Jesus has other plans. Several times Jesus has cryptically prophesied his own death on a cross (16:21; 17:22).

Why do you think Moses and Elijah appeared with Jesus? What would be the significance of these two OT figures being represented at the Transfiguration?

Lateral Contexts

Read Mk 9:33-37 and Lk 9:46-48 Matthew includes some of the Markan material, but is clearly intent on giving his readers the full discourse by Jesus on the issue of "who is the greatest?" The humility and vulnerability of a child is present in both the Mark and Matthew material.

Note: Mark and Luke portray the disciples as having an internal squabble that Jesus has to break into, while Matthew portrays the disciples as initiating the discussion with Jesus. Also, Luke mentions that Jesus read their innermost thoughts, while Matthew puts the question on the lips of the disciples. It is interesting that Matthew's details about the argument are greatly abbreviated and compressed, but the discourse Jesus gave them is greatly expanded. This abbreviated setup shows that Matthew was intent on leaving ample room for the actual teachings and sayings of Jesus.

Also read, Lk 15:4-7 for Luke's exposition on the Lost sheep.

Theological Contexts
Proverbs 11:2 states, "When pride comes, then comes disgrace. But with humility comes wisdom."

Read Phil 2:1-11. What does Paul state about having an attitude of humility here?

Col 3:12 teaches us to clothe ourselves with humility among other virtues. What is the difference between this kind of humble disposition and meekness and the false humility that Paul speaks of in Col 2:18?

Broadening Your Perspective

Considering the Inherited Culture (the OT)
How does the Old Testament factor into Jesus' teaching on Community Rules?
There is an unmistakable inference to Ps 23 in Jesus' statement regarding the "lost sheep" of Israel.[40] Like Jn chapter 10, this passage also evokes the imagery of the false shepherds of Ezekiel 34 in contrast to the coming Shepherd of Israel. The Ezekiel passage is characterized by 2 things: first, God states that he himself will be Israel's shepherd. And, second, this shepherd would come from the line of David, which fits the Messianic motif of Matthew.

Considering the Immediate Culture
What significance does the culture of the New Testament have on this passage?
Keener states, "Ancient moralists regularly trotted forth models of heroes and statesmen for their students to imitate; Jesus instead points to a child."[41] Also, it is clear that other Messianic sects included certain "rules" for resolving conflict and seeking reconciliation through mediation and multiple witnesses.[42]

---

40 Blomberg, *Commentary on the New Testament*, 56.

41 Keener, *A Socio-Rhetorical Commentary*, 447.

42 Blomberg, *Commentary on the New Testament*, 57.

Journaling for Practical Application

Reflect on the Jesus countercultural view of forgiveness and reconciliation. Answer the following:

Is there anyone in your life now that you need to go and be reconciled with in this manner? Write out your thoughts and prayers for that person.

_____

_____

_____

_____

_____

_____

_____

Take a moment to think about humility.

Would you describe yourself as a person who humbles themselves often, or is your view of "greatness" different? How does Jesus' example and teaching regarding humility effect the way you think on a day to day basis?

_____

_____

_____

_____

_____

_____

The parable of the wicked servant and the forgiving King shows us what about God's view of forgiveness?

_____

_____

_____

_____

_____

The 5 Discourses cont... Week 9

Discourse Number 5: Jesus' Final Challenge - It's the End of the World as They Know It!

Introduction: Jesus makes his way toward the Mount of Olives and the disciples call his attention to the magnificence of the Herodian architecture surrounding the temple complex (24:1). Much to their surprise, Jesus launches into a prophetic denunciation of the Temple as he had previously done to their rabbinic luminaries in chapter twenty three. He then finishes his speech with a series of short stories that graphically illustrate their need to stay faithful, watchful, and act mercifully toward each other and the world while the Master is away.

Read Chapters 24-25:

In 24:1-2, What do the disciples draw Jesus' attention to? The disciples appear to be very impressed by the Herodian architecture. What is Jesus' response to their amazement at these sacred structures?

The disciples ask Jesus two questions that precipitate Jesus' response. What are they (v. 3)?

Though Jesus is clearly using OT apocalyptic imagery (end of the world language) in this discourse, how is his use of this imagery different than his previous mode of speaking in parables (particularly ch. 24)?

The prophetic outburst of Jesus is followed by three parables in chapter 25: In light of chapter 24, what seems to be the main point of each of them?

•The ten virgins:

•The talents:

•The sheep and the goats:

Immediate Contexts

According to Matthew, the final discourse comes on the heels of Jesus having just denounced the Pharisees and scribes as "hypocrites." He tells the disciples that they are to avoid the honored title *rabbi* and that they were not to be called "teacher for they had but one teacher, the Christ" (23:10). Reminiscent of Jeremiah, he then grieves over the Jews' rejection of him and states that their house is left "desolate." Jesus has gone from the heights of popularity and now senses his looming rejection and the subsequent trial for his disciples that these events will pose.[43]

Lateral Contexts

Read Mk 13 and Luke 21. In particular, how does Luke appear to paraphrase this Sermon? Why do you think his Olivet Discourse looks so different than Matthew's?

As you compare Mk 13:14-23 and Lk 21:20-24, how do these authors explain the "great tribulation" in a similar or different way?

Luke's Jesus does not quote the OT explicitly. Instead, Luke portrays Jesus as greatly paraphrasing the OT passages. Why do you think Luke does this?

---

43 Wilkins, "Matthew," 769-770.

Theological Contexts

Read Dan 12:6. In what ways does Daniel also have questions about the sequence and timing of the end?[44]

Read Dan 9:27. How does Jesus seem to allude to this imagery in his "Abomination of Desolation" language (Mt 24:15)?

In 1 Thess 4:16-18, Paul speaks of the coming of the Lord. How does Paul portray his coming in this passage?

---

44 Blomberg, *Commentary on the New Testament,* 86-87.

In 2 Thess 2:1-12, Paul appears to pick up on this theme of the "man of lawlessness" and the one doomed to destruction. How does Paul speak of the end in these passages?

When you read Rev 13:1-11, in what ways does this seem to parallel 2 Thess 2:3-4 and Rev. 13?

Broadening Your Perspective

Considering the Inherited Culture (the OT)
How does the Old Testament factor into Jesus' teaching on the end?
Jesus draws from several Old Testament passages. He uses the prophetic language of cosmic upheaval quoting from Isaiah 13:10 and 34:4. Jesus also alludes to Dan 7, 9, and 12, and once refers to the story of Noah as an analogy of his coming.
The only language appropriate to explain what it will be like to be on the wrong side of God's judgment is this kind of graphic imagery regarding "the sun being darkened and the moon will not give its light..." etc. In the text, Jesus is assuming the role of apocalyptic "prophet," "Messiah," "Son of Man," and their "Lord (24: 30, 36).

Considering the Immediate Culture
What significance does the culture of the New Testament have on this passage?
Daniel's prophecy of the "Seven" in 9:27 was interpreted variously by Jews prior to Jesus. A fairly specific parallel to Jesus' usage would be the 1 Maccabees 1:54 passage which interpreted Daniel as being fulfilled in the destruction of the Temple under Antiochus Epiphanes in 167-164 BC.[45] It must be remembered that Jesus' response is an answer to the disciples' two questions (when will this happen and what is the sign...). These are issues that every Jewish male wrestled with when they read prophecies such as Dan 7 and 9 and 12.[46]

Summary: The five discourses establish Jesus' authority to teach and train them. Jesus' instructions are intensely practical guidelines for their worship, community, service, Kingdom life, and watchfulness in anticipation of the Master's return. The entire Gospel is framed by Jesus' own emphasis on the importance of applying his teaching (Mt 7:24ff.) and Jesus authorizing his disciples to make disciples by "teaching them..." (28:19).

---

45 Blomberg, *Commentary on the New Testament*, 86. Antiochus Epiphanes was a Greek King who desecrated the temple a century before Jesus' time.

46 Keener, *A Socio-Rhetorical Commentary*, 447.

Journaling for Practical Application

Take a few lines to reflect on Jesus' ultimate return to earth in power.

How often do you think about the coming of Jesus? Based on some of the passages you read, what do you think that time will be like for disciples of Jesus?

_____
_____
_____
_____
_____
_____
_____
_____
_____
_____
_____
_____
_____

Take a moment to respond to Jesus parables in Matthew 25:

Would you describe yourself as a "watchful" person (25:1-13)? What does it mean for you to have your "lamp" ready for the Master's return?

_____
_____
_____
_____
_____
_____
_____

When you consider the parable of the talents in 25:14-30, what kind of investment has Jesus made in your life? How has he gifted you to serve in his Kingdom?

_____

_____

_____

_____

_____

_____

In what ways specifically are you endeavoring to make good on God's investment of time, resources and opportunities in your life? In what ways do you feel that you could improve here?

_____

_____

_____

_____

_____

_____

_____

_____

Jesus specifically identified the good sheep as those who met the practical needs of others in service (25:31-46). In what ways are you personally challenged to reach out to others through the giving of resources?

_____

_____

_____

_____

_____

_____

Interactions with Peter Week 10

Introduction: Simon Peter is easily the most prominent figure in the NT other than Jesus himself. There are 210 references to Peter (including those in the Epistles) compared to 162 references to Paul and 142 of the other disciples all together.[47] Though it may be argued that Peter appears prominently because of his leadership role in the early church, it is almost certain that Peter's story also serves as an example for disciples in general (both positive and negative aspects).[48]

Read the Following:

In 4:18, Peter is called to discipleship by Jesus. What kind of commitment did following Jesus involve for these original disciples?

What play on words does Jesus use when he calls these disciples?

---

47 Wilkins, *Following the Master*, 152.

48 Wilkins, *Following the Master*, 154.

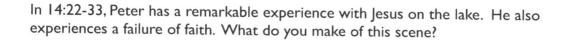

In 14:22-33, Peter has a remarkable experience with Jesus on the lake. He also experiences a failure of faith. What do you make of this scene?

Reading 16:13-16, Jesus asks the all important question that every disciple must answer. "Who do you say that I am?" How does Peter speak up and voice the disciples belief in Jesus?

Over in 17:1-8, Peter experienced the most remarkable and dramatic encounter with Jesus that a person could have this side of eternity. Why do you think that Jesus only took Peter, James, and John to see him transfigured like this?

What is Peter's response to Jesus' self-revelation of his glory?

In 18:21-35, Peter suggests that he should forgive his brother "up to seven times" which would easily exceed the rabbinic consensus on the matter.[49] But Jesus blows him away with a parable on forgiveness. Do you think that this was a misstep by Peter to bring this up?

Lastly, in 26:69-75, Peter experiences the bitter failure of denying his Lord. What is Jesus' response to Peter when it was all said and done (Jn 21:15-19)?

Summary: Peter experienced the full gamut of successes and failures in his discipleship experience. He is called by the master to leave his harsh and difficult life of fishing the waters of Galilee to a life of learning and apprenticeship with Jesus. He shows initiative and wonder as he steps out of the boat. Then, he simultaneously prevails and falters in his faith. He experiences the heights of commendation for his inspired confession and then experiences the depths of reprimand for failing to understand the true nature of Jesus' Messianic mission. He is privy'd to an unprecedented disclosure of Jesus' glory followed by blundering uncertainty. This is followed by Peter's premature flexing as he learns the principle of "forgiveness with no fine print" from Jesus. Lastly, Peter's betrayal is a bitter pill that can only be made right by the grace of Jesus after his resurrection.

---

49 Wilkins, "Matthew," 622.

Exploring the Context

Immediate Contexts

• As you look at the end of chapter 4, it appears that Jesus is growing in popularity. He is healing the sick, casting out demon spirits, and is gaining a massive following from the surrounding regions. This helps make sense of why the disciples would have left everything to follow him on such short notice.

• Leading up to chapter 14, Jesus has shown himself to be the Supreme arbiter and teacher of God's word (ch's 5-7), to wield an unprecedented power over disease, illness, and demons (4; 8-9; 11:20-24; 12:15-20), and he has routed the teachers and religious experts with his superior logic and argumentation (12:1-14; 22-45). Now, in chapter 14, he shows himself to be the Lord over nature and the elements. Peter's belief in Jesus is warranted by what he's seen and heard from the master so far.

• In chapter 16, Peter realizes, by the Spirit, that Jesus is the Messiah. However, to this point, they have only understood the purpose of the Messiah through their cultural lenses. But from chapter 16 on, Jesus begins to reveal the suffering servant mission of the Christ (16:21).

- In chapter 17, Peter, James, and John see the glorified Lord with Moses and Elijah. Yet, in chapters 12 and 16, the Pharisees, Sadducees and Torah teachers demand a sign from Jesus. They want him to provide Messianic credentials. Jesus refuses to reveal himself to these doubters, but then reveals the greatest sign to his disciples (his transfiguration), who have just confessed their faith in him (ch 16).

- Ironically, Peter will learn the forgiveness principle of chapter 18 the hard way. Peter must forgive those who have seized and executed his master, just as the Master forgave his incalculable debt of betrayal.

Lateral Contexts

- Read Mt 10:2-4; Mk 3:16-19; Lk 6:14-16; Ac 1:13. Who appears first in the list of Apostles and Disciples from these passages?[50]

---

50 Wilkins, *Following the Master*, 153.

- Read Jn 6:66-69. How does John tell the story of Peter's confession as spokesman for the other disciples?

- Read Ac 1-2. How does Peter seem to change after he is filled with the Spirit?

- In Ac 8, Peter is instrumental in opening the door of the Gospel to the Samaritans. In Ac 10, Peter is instrumental in bringing the Gospel of Jesus to the gentiles. It seems that Peter was indeed given the "keys" (Mt 16:19) to unlocking these doors of opportunity to the rest of the world. In this way, Peter serves a foundational role in the life of the early church.[51]

---

51 Wilkins, *Following the Master*, 154.

- In Gal 2, Paul has a confrontation with Peter. What is the nature of this conflict?

- In 1 Cor 9:5, Peter obviously continued to establish and strengthen churches around the world.

Theological Contexts

In Mt 16:18, Jesus states, "you are Peter. And on this rock I will build my church, and the gates of hell will not overcome it."

The first theological emphasis on Peter is his foundational role in the building of Jesus' church. Mt 16 and 18 are the only places in the Gospels where the Greek word *ecclesia*, meaning "church" is used. Matthew reflects on Jesus' promise to establish his church, partly on the foundation of Peter's statement (Jesus is the "Christ"), and partly by means of Peter's commission to unlock the Gospel message to Judea, Samaria, and the ends of the earth (Ac 1, 6, 10-12). On the day of Pentecost, Jesus establishes his church (assembly) to bring the Gospel to the world. Though the church began like a mustard seed (a fledgling sect of Judaism on the perimeter of the Roman empire) they would eventually spread into the world proclaiming that Jesus is the world's true Lord and Caesar's Kingdom is a sham.[52]

The second theological emphasis on Peter worth noting is his representational role among the disciples. Wilkins notes, "Matthew has portrayed a very realistic picture of the person Peter. He is not some mythical or *midrashic* caricature, but a very real disciple whom Jesus has personally taught, corrected, and established as a rock to carry on his work...That Peter is not some kind of 'supreme rabbi' is indicated by the fact that he does not always represent the disciples in a positive way"[53]

52 NT Wright, *Jesus and the Victory of God* (Minneapolis: Fortress Press, 1996), 610.

53 Michael Wilkins, *Discipleship in the Ancient World and Matthew's Gospel* (Baker Books: Grand Rapids, 1992), 210.

Broadening Your Perspective

Considering the Inherited Culture (the OT)
How does the Old Testament factor into Peter's narrative?
The incident in Mt 16:15-20 likely contains several OT references. Ps 118:22 refers to the "stone" the builders discarded becoming the capstone. This imagery as the "rock" or a foundational stone is a rich image (Is 28:15-19). It is also possible that Jesus' use of this imagery for Peter could refer back to Is 51:1-2, thus "making Peter a founding father of the New Covenant community."[54]

Considering the Immediate Culture
What significance does the culture of the New Testament have on this passage?
In the rabbinic culture "binding and loosing" was the purview of the learned scholar.[55] Based on precedent, the teacher would pronounce binding legal rulings in matters of *Halakah* (from the Hebrew word meaning "the way"). Likewise, the scribe was an executor of legal and judicial matters and some even educated children in the local synagogues.[56] Though it is clear that Peter and the other Apostles will have a similar role in Jesus' new movement, it seems that the controlling metaphor is of a "building" with a "foundation" and "gates" that need to be unlocked.[57] Thus, Jesus raids the vocabulary of his rabbinic counterparts but applies it differently. The language for Peter would simply mean that his ministry will be instrumental in unlocking the Gospel concentrically from Jerusalem to the nations.[58] This would involve both Peter and the Apostles' authoritative teaching (binding and loosing) concerning Jesus, as well as Peter's apostolic validation of God's work in new frontiers of Gospel ministry (Jerusalem, Judea, Samaria, and the ends of the earth).

---

54 Blomberg, *Commentary on the New Testament*, 55.

55 Wilkins, *Following the Master*, 366.

56 Craig S. Keener, *A Commentary on the Gospel of Matthew* (Grand Rapids: Eerdmans, 1999), 53.

57 Wilkins, "Matthew," 567.

58 Wilkins, "Matthew," 567.

Conclusion: On the one hand, Peter's experience as a disciple captures the typical ebb and flow of the believer's growth. The various peaks and valleys of Peter's life were instructive for Matthew's own community. Peter serves partially as an exemplar of what it means to be a disciple of Jesus: allowed to succeed and fail on the Master's watch. However, Matthew's portrayal is also a historical snap shot, that is, there were many gaps in the disciple's understanding. After Pentecost, the Spirit would enable each believer to follow the Master with an unprecedented power for living. It is noteworthy that Peter's "track record" gets remarkably better after Pentecost.

Reflect on Peter's experience as a disciple? Answer the following:

With chapter 4 in mind, can you recall what it was like when you first met Jesus? Write down some reflections regarding your own experience with Jesus' call to discipleship.

_____

_____

_____

_____

_____

_____

_____

Take a moment to comment on your own personal revelation of Jesus as Lord.

Jesus said that "flesh and blood" had not revealed the truth of Jesus to Peter. What was your experience like? Can you remember that moment when you just knew that Jesus is the Christ and you believed on him for salvation?

_____

_____

_____

_____

_____

Recall an instance in your own life when, like Peter, you seemed to have boundless faith. What was your experience like trying to "walk" on the impossible? Did you experience a failure of faith as well? Reflect on Jesus' grace to you in the midst of both faith and faltering.

_____

_____

_____

_____

_____

_____

_____

_____

_____

_____

_____

_____

Reflecting on Jesus' interaction with Peter in chapter 18, have you ever had a spiritually mature brother or sister correct you (especially when you thought you had it figured out)? What was that like? Did you take the correction well?

_____

_____

_____

_____

_____

_____

_____

Peter would need forgiveness later after denying Christ. How have you experienced the forgiveness and mercy of Jesus in your own life? Can you think of anyone you need to forgive right now in your heart?

_____

_____

_____

_____

_____

_____

_____

Confrontation with Leaders Week 11

Engaging the Text

Introduction: Matthew depicts the religious leaders who opposed Jesus as smug, self-righteous, and hypocritical people. In a sense, these pious clerics and rabbinic pundits were like anti-Jesus'. They appeared to be very righteous but this was nothing more than a religious veneer of piety. In the process of confronting their superficial devotion, Jesus actually taught all of his disciples how **not** to act.

Read the Following:

In 9:1-8, Jesus confronted the religious pundits who silently heckled him from the "peanut gallery." Jesus hears their evil thoughts. What point is the Savior making to these religious experts?

In the very next story, the Pharisees can hardly believe that Jesus is fraternizing with "sinners" and people of ill-repute. What is Jesus' response to that in verses 12-13?

Later in this same chapter (9:34 and 12:24), Jesus is confronted by these pious clerics who make an accusation that the source of his miracles was the evil one. How does Jesus deal with this claim? How serious of an issue was it for them to claim that his "spirit" was an evil one?

In 12:2-14, the Pharisees make the allegation that Jesus is not Sabbath-compliant (he's broken their sabbath rules). How does Jesus correct this overemphasis on external religion (12:3)?

Several times in the Matthew story Jesus is challenged to produce miraculous credentials (12:38; 16:1). Does Jesus oblige them? How does Jesus face this challenge for miraculous accreditation?

Read 15:1-20. Here, the Jews accuse him of ritual impurity. Jesus and the disciples had ignored the purity traditions of the Pharisees and teacher of the law. In 15:3, what does Jesus say is the most important "law" to keep? How would this offend a pious teacher in that culture?

In 19:3-12, the Pharisees tested Jesus with a question about divorce. Obviously wanting him to take their side on this controversial issue, they wanted to know why He would take a position that would supersede Moses' own command in the Torah. What does Jesus appeal to?

How does this show Jesus' self-awareness of His own authority to teach God's word?

Read 22:15-22. The Pharisees sent their disciples and the Herodians (from Herod's party) to Jesus to question him on paying taxes to Caesar. This interrogation lead to their humiliation. How so?

Now read 22:23-33. The Sadducees (another religious sect) tested Jesus with a very clever riddle that apparently none of their Pharasaic opponents could solve. How does Jesus embarrass them? What does Jesus say they are ignorant of?

A sad and final confrontation appears in chapter 23, but this time it is initiated by Jesus assuming the role of Israel's prophet. Read the whole chapter. What are some words that Jesus repeats throughout this chapter? What does he call the Pharisees and Torah Teachers?

Summary: Jesus fearlessly confronted the wrong-headed religious culture of his time. He teaches his disciples through these encounters that a fixation on external piety (divorced from the heart), ritualistic purity, and hypocritical living results in a defective and fraudulent spirituality. Disciples are to avoid the "yeast" of the Pharisees and Sadducees at all costs.

Exploring the Context

Immediate Contexts

Just prior to Jesus' confrontation with the Pharisees, Teachers of the Law, and Sadducees, Matthew takes pains to tell us that Jesus' miracle working ministry was qualitatively superior to other would-be messianic figures. Initially, it is easy to see how Jesus would have been popular with both the crowd and the religious clerics. Yet, Matthew shows us an increasing pattern of escalation between Jesus and the teachers. At first, Jesus merely corrects them when he is put to the test. But ultimately, Jesus rejects and denounces them prophetically.

Lateral Contexts

• Read Mk 2:1-12 and Lk 5:17-26 for similar accounts of the healing of the Paralytic and the rebuke of the experts in the Law.

• Read Mk 2:23-28 and Lk 6:1-5. How is Jesus the Lord of the sabbath? Why would this saying be offensive?

• Lk 11:29-32 shows Jesus challenging them with the sign of Jonah. In Mt 12:38-42; 16:1-4, Jesus tells them a similar thing. Why would Jesus not comply and show them signs on demand?

- Read Mk 7:1-23. Matthew maintains much of Marks material in 15:1-20. How does Jesus put the emphasis on internal righteousness in these two passages?

- In Mt 19:3-12, Jesus teaches that if someone divorces his wife and marries another (except for unfaithfulness) then he commits adultery. Yet, in Mk 10:2-12, Jesus does not include the caveat for "unfaithfulness." What is your take on that?

- See Mk 12:13-17 and Lk 20:19-26 for Jesus' challenge regarding paying taxes to Caesar (Mt 22:15-22).

- Read Mk 12:38-40 and Lk 20:45-47 regarding Jesus' warning against pharisees found in Mt 23. Why do think the other Gospel writers abbreviated this confrontation so dramatically? Why would Matthew include so much material for his Jewish audience?

Theological Contexts

It seems that in every age, the church must face this insidious threat to the Gospel of God's mercy and grace. The greatest threat to the faith is not postmodernism, secularism, or Islam. The greatest threat to the Christian faith is not **foreign** religion, but rather **familiar** religion. It is the temptation to subtly alter the DNA of grace, mutating into a form of godliness that denies the power of the Gospel.

Broadening Your Perspective

Considering the Inherited Culture (the OT)

How does the Old Testament factor into Jesus' confrontation with the Religious leaders?
Matthew depicts the Pharisees and the Teachers of the Law as the very people that Isaiah prophesied about. In fact, Paul himself was dogged by the "Judaizers" who constantly undermined his efforts among the churches by advocating the Works of Torah along with Christ (Gal 3). As well, Matthew's Gospel was likely written during a period when the Pharasaic branch of Judaism was on the rise and on its way to becoming the surviving sect among the Jews.

Considering the Immediate Culture

What significance does the culture of the New Testament have on these texts?
We must keep in mind that prior to the destruction of the temple (AD 70), religious training existed in a more *formative* state - meaning that the rabbinic academies had not been *formalized* in Jesus' day. However, Jews were considered among the most educated people in the ancient world because of their homeschooling and their informal synagogue education.

In addition to this general emphasis on scribal learning and rabbinic ministry, there existed unusually charismatic leaders who functioned as "wisdom sages." Craig Keener notes, "It is true that Jesus was not part of what later became the rabbinic movement, nor was he merely a Jewish scribe or ancient Near Eastern wisdom sage. However, many early sages traveled, and it is unlikely that most Galilean Jews who saw themselves as faithful to God's law would have sharply contrasted charismatic teachers from other teachers of the law as if the former lacked legal wisdom. Most scholars note that many characteristics of Jesus' ministry fit expectations for sages and scribes, and whatever else Jesus may have been, he was clearly a Jewish teacher of one or both types as well."[59]

Functioning as a charismatic wisdom sage, Jesus would easily gain followers with varying degrees of devotion. Like his contemporaries: Honi the Circle Drawer, Hanina ben Dosa, Jochanan ben Zakkai, and Simon bar Kochba, Jesus would attract a crowd of followers who would come to venerate him as an important figure.[60] Unlike these rabbis, he would

---

59 Keener, *The Gospel of Matthew: A Socio-Rhetorical Commentary,* 54. Keener refers to the fact that the ordained rabbi (Tannaim 70-200 AD) did not formerly exist until after the destruction of the temple and Jerusalem in AD 70. Although many of the later rabbinic traditions formalized at that time likely existed in some informal way during the 2nd Temple period of Jesus' day.

60 Flavius Josephus, *Jewish Antiquities*, book XX (Great Britain: Wordsworth Editions, 2006), 866-867. Additionally, Josephus lists many would-be messiah's who were met with the iron hand of Roman suppression.

attract followers in the tens of thousands instead of just a few hundred. This is likely due to his unparalleled miraculous power.[61]

Conclusion: Disciples should avoid the "yeast" of cynicism, religious externalism, and majoring in minor details of religious observance. This is especially true for pious "traditions" of men that are not explicitly grounded in Scripture. Hypocrisy and self-righteousness are intolerable qualities for a genuine disciple of Jesus.

61 However, questions regarding with whom Jesus had apprenticed do surface later on (Jn. 7:15ff). Jesus' opponents are dumbfounded that he teaches with authority, knowledge, and wisdom, without quoting previous rabbinic rulings and without having formally studied in the rabbinic academies. Jesus' response is that his *halakhic* (הלכה) authority is from God alone and not a rabbinic school. Sigal mentions that Jesus' rejection of the Pharisees *halakhic* authority was most definitely a bold counter-offensive against a corrupt *purishim*, see Phillip Sigal, *The Hallakah of Jesus* (Atlanta: SBL, 2000), 143.

Reflect on the following:

Mt 6 and chapter 23, Jesus' uses the pejorative "hypocrite" to describe these men. How does Jesus warn us against this character flaw?

_____

_____

_____

_____

_____

_____

_____

_____

_____

How do believers today sometimes get trapped by the temptation of religious externalism? How about you? Write some specific instances in your life when you've struggled with this?

_____

_____

_____

_____

_____

_____

_____

Lastly, how do we have a tendency to create additional "rules" that obscure the core message of Jesus' Gospel?

_____

_____

_____

Interruptions From the Crowd ⌒ Week 12

Engaging the Text

Introduction: So far, we have learned discipleship principles and commands from the five sermons of Jesus, and we have learned how *not* to behave and think from Jesus' interactions with the Pharisees and teachers. Now we turn our attention to those in the crowd who have essentially sought Jesus out to receive something from him. In each of these cases, Jesus teaches critical discipleship truths.

Read the Following Stories Carefully Noting These Points of Emphasis:

The Leper (8:1-4): How does Jesus touch the untouchable?

The Centurion (8:5-13): How does Jesus show that a person's faith is more valuable than religious pedigree?

The Paralytic (9:1-8): The Son of Man has authority to forgive and heal?

The Dead Girl and the Hemophiliac (9:18-26): How does Jesus touch those who are off limits?

The Canaanite Woman (15:21-28): How does the woman's persistence in faith trump religious heritage?

The Epileptic Boy (17:14-21): In what way were the disciples ineffective?

The Little Children (19:13-15): How does the Kingdom belong to the "childlike?"

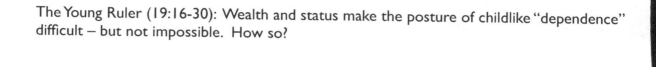

The Young Ruler (19:16-30): Wealth and status make the posture of childlike "dependence" difficult – but not impossible. How so?

The Two Blind Men (20:29-34): How does the story illustrate that Jesus' delays aren't denials?

Summary: Disciples are to emulate the way that Jesus reached out to untouchable people, prioritized faith over religious heritage, and exhibited a humble dependence on God.

Immediate Contexts

- Matthew's Gospel is punctuated with many occasions where Jesus ministered to the crowd (Gk. *ochloi*). This ministry is often "interrupted" by a specific request from someone.[62] Matthew characterizes the crowd as largely a faithless but fascinated group of Christ-admirers. Some who come out of the crowd actually demonstrate their faith in him and so become Christ-followers in a metaphysical or spiritual sense.[63] So the faith and submission of the leper and the Roman centurion is followed by a scribe and an unnamed disciple who also come out of the crowd. Yet, Jesus points out that they can not be his disciples unless they are willing to embrace the hardships of his itinerate ministry (8:18-22).

- Additionally, when Jesus heals the paralytic, he is immediately challenged by the Scribes and Pharisees. They challenge his authority to forgive sins, his associations with known sinners, and his non-compliance with trivial rules of Jewish observance (9:3-14). Yet, in spite of the opposition from the religious leaders, a synagogue ruler is brave enough to kneel before him in faith. Matthew then offers a summative paragraph, reflecting on the overwhelming scope of the needs: *the harvest is plentiful, but the laborers are few* (9:35-38).

---

62 Wilkins, *Discipleship in the Ancient World*, 170-172.

63 Wilkins, *Discipleship in the Ancient World*, 170.

- Though it appeared at first that Jesus' miraculous ministry would be the centerpiece of his mission, chapters 16 and 17 mark an important turning point in the story. Jesus is now beginning to warn his disciples of his primary mission and objective as Messiah: he must be betrayed and put to death by his own people (16:21; 17:9). The miracle of curing the epileptic boy (17:14-21) is flanked by many cryptic and chilling predictions of his eventual death on a cross.

- Because Jesus is moving ever closer to Jerusalem, and because he has revealed himself in glory accompanied by Moses and Elijah (17), certainly his disciples expected him to reveal himself as the glorified Davidic Messiah. This expectation gives an opportunity for the disciples' petty squabbling over which of them will be the greatest (18). Yet, Jesus turns their attention to the community rules of forgiveness that should govern their interactions when he is gone.

- Jesus must then correct the disciples' understanding of the nature of his Kingdom. Jesus' Kingdom will be a place where those who show childlike dependence on him will enter and reign with him (19:13-15). This illustration of the little children coming to be blessed is then followed by a wealthy young man who finds it too difficult to adopt a humble, dependent posture toward Jesus (19:16-29). This entire "interruption" is surprisingly not absorbed by the disciples. For, James and John are caught in the embarrassing situation of trying to posture themselves as co-rulers (20:17-19), all while Jesus is trying to warn them of his impending death and resurrection.

- Lastly, it seems that Jesus' miraculous ministry among the crowds is spinning out (20:29-34). The text makes it clear that the two blind men called out to Jesus several times. In fact, Matthew seems to indicate that Jesus only responded to them after several attempts to shout over the crowds. Though Jesus seems focussed on his mission, he nevertheless is moved with compassion and heals the blind men who began to follow him. This incident is followed by the height of Jesus' popularity among the crowds. Yet Jesus must "cleanse" or symbolize the obsolescence of the Temple as a proper dwelling of God (21:1-17). This incident escalates the conflict between Jesus and the Pharisees.

Lateral Contexts
Though we can't cover them all, let's zoom in on a few parallel passages to the stories above.

- The Leper (8:1-4): Read also Mk 1:40-45, and Lk 5:12-16

- The Centurion (8:5-13): Read also Lk 7:1-10

- The Paralytic (9:1-8): Read also Mk 2:1-10, Lk 5:17

- The Dead Girl and the Hemophiliac (9:18-26): Mk 5:21-43, and Lk 8:40-56

- The Little Children (19:13-15): Mk 10:13-16, and Lk 18:15-17

- The Young Ruler (19:16-29): Mk 10:17-31, and Lk 18:18-30

- The Two Blind Men (20:29-34): (Note that this is the last miracle among the crowds in Matthew). Mk 10:46-52, and read Lk 18:35-43.

Note how each Gospel emphasizes various aspects of the story offering a compelling and complimentary perspective on these events.

Theological Contexts

Jesus' miraculous ministry began in "Galilee of the Gentiles." The people living in darkness have seen a great light. Jesus is the Wonderful Counselor, Everlasting Father, Prince of Peace who will take his place to dispense God's justice to Israel and the nations.[64] But before he can take his rightful place as the permanent judge and ruler of the political Kingdoms of our world, he must first minister healing, justice, and mercy to the crowds - *first to the Jews and then to the Gentiles.* Though the crowds are the object of Jesus' miraculous activity, they eventually will be turned and will unwittingly perform Isaiah's suffering servant motif (Is 53:7).[65] The New Testament disciples will continue Jesus' ministry of grace and healing to the crowds, and Paul himself will be the instrument to usher the Good News to the nations (Rom 1:10).

---

64 Blomberg, *Commentary on the New Testament*, 18.

65 Wilkins, *Discipleship in the Ancient World*, 170-172.

Broadening Your Perspective

Considering the Inherited Culture (the OT)
How does the Old Testament factor into Jesus' ministry to the crowds?
See the theological context above.

Considering the Immediate Culture
What significance does the culture of the New Testament have on these texts?
3 factors must be considered when reading of Jesus' ministry to the harassed and helpless crowds:
1) The crowds were expecting a largely political Davidic warrior. The notion of the suffering servant of Isaiah was not the controlling narrative of their time.[66]
2) The crowds were viewed as pawns in a larger political game that suffused the theological landscape of Israel. There were groups that were overtly political e.g. the Herodians and the Sadducees. Theological concerns were certainly secondary, or at least inextricably linked to political realities for them.
However, even the Pharisees were a political group to a degree. Though they sought religious and spiritual reform of the people, this was yet another control mechanism to sway the crowds over to their political viewpoint. They were the "defacto political leaders" in Israel.[67]
3) Jesus offered the crowds the messianic shepherding they so desperately needed (and were without), yet the crowds chose the path of political revolution, which Jesus warned them against (Mt 24).

---

66 NT Wright, *The New Testament and the People of God* (Fortress Press: Minneapolis, 1992), 319-321.

67 Wright, *The New Testament and the People of God*, 187. Wright mentions that "...the power they wielded, though in modern terms religious in origin and intent, was emphatically political in effect."

Reflect on the various "interruptions" of those seeking healing and mercy from Jesus. Answer the following:
Can you imagine how it must have felt to be an untouchable leper in that society? Write down some people you think exist in our culture today who would be "modern lepers." What do you think the church's response should be to them?

_____
_____
_____
_____
_____
_____
_____
_____
_____
_____
_____
_____
_____
_____

Take a moment to comment on Jesus' forgiveness of the paralytic in chapter 9.
Why do you think Jesus forgave his sin first before healing his body?

_____
_____
_____
_____
_____
_____
_____

Recall an instance in your own life when your faith caused you to take drastic steps toward Jesus?

_____

_____

_____

_____

_____

_____

_____

_____

_____

Jesus sees the paralytic's faith. What lesson about "demonstrated faith" might Matthew be emphasizing to future disciples here? How specifically can you *show* Jesus your own faith?

_____

_____

_____

_____

_____

_____

_____

_____

On two occasions, Jesus welcomed children and either blessed them or held their child-like humility up as an example for the disciples. Take a moment and reflect on that.

How might we look more like the rich young man who went away sad? Is there anything in your life that has your allegiance over following the Master? If so, write it down and pray about it?

As you assess your "child-like quotient," how do you stack up? Is there anything specifically that Jesus would "tweak" about your own humility factor?

_____

_____

Stages of Development Week 13

Engaging the Text

Introduction: To this point, we have discovered that Matthew's Gospel works as a virtual handbook on discipleship. Not only does Jesus have much to say regarding discipleship in five major teachings, but he has also taught his disciples through his interactions with his opponents, the crowds, and those who have come out of the crowds to express faith in him. We now zoom in on the process of training the twelve in order to gain insights about how Jesus trains future disciples.

One Caution: We must be careful to take note of those discontinuous aspects of the disciples' training. Meaning, that Jesus trained and equipped the twelve disciples to fulfill a leadership role giving them certain apostolic prerogatives and responsibilities. However there is a general pattern of training that we must translate to our own experience now that Christ abides with each of us through the agency of the Spirit.

Read:

The Calling of Disciples
Mt 4:18-23. The vocation of a disciple is to "fish" for the souls of men.

Read Mt 9:9-13. Jesus calls unlikely people to follow and be trained as his disciples - even those considered to be off limits.

Read Mt 10:1ff. The nature of the disciples' ministry and being called to this special role (as the twelve) was proclaiming the Gospel in the power of the Spirit.

Summary: The Disciples **were called** by the Master: Disciples respond to the Spirit's conviction and calling through the preaching of the Word.

Disciples Follow and Understand the Master
Mt 4:20 states that the disciples left their nets "immediately and followed him." This implies more than a change of vocation, or literally following him from town to town. This implies an existential identification with the Messiah's cause. Disciples choose to move into an exclusive commitment to Jesus as the Master.

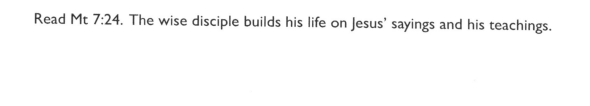

Read Mt 7:24. The wise disciple builds his life on Jesus' sayings and his teachings.

In Mt 13:51, Jesus asks them if they have "understood all these things?" The disciples answer "yes."

In Mt 16:12, Jesus challenges the disciples to beware of the "yeast" of the Pharisees and Sadducees. At first, they misunderstand the metaphor, but then clearly understand that Jesus is referring to the teaching of the Pharisees and Sadducees.

Summary: The Disciples **followed and understood** the Master: Disciples commit themselves to knowing Christ's teaching and His way of life (revealed in Scripture). The Disciples **learned** from the Masters yoke of teaching: They build their lives on the solid foundation of Jesus by application of His Word in the power of the Spirit.

Disciples are Empowered to Preach the Gospel

We read in chapter 10 that Jesus commissioned the disciples to go first to the Jews and empowered them to proclaim the message.

In Mt 28:19-20, Jesus authorized his followers to make more disciples by teaching them to obey all that he'd commanded.

Summary: Jesus **empowered** his disciples for service: Disciples utilize their spiritual gifts in service to the Master – learning to succeed and fail on the Master's watch. Jesus **authorized** his followers to make disciples of the nations: They are empowered and authorized to convert their neighbors through incarnational ministry and apologetics.

Conclusion: Matthews' Gospel introduces us to many critical aspects of discipleship to Jesus. The Gospel begins by establishing Jesus' identity and then asserting his authority to interpret and to arbitrate God's word. Throughout the Gospel, Jesus teaches his **disciples**, his **antagonists**, and the **crowd**. He instructs everyone through his direct teaching and his example. The Gospel ends with the risen Jesus authorizing his followers to continue his mission of making disciples — teaching them to observe all that he'd commanded them (in word and deed).

Journaling for Practical Application

Reflect on the disciple's experience as they literally followed Jesus around from town to town.

How do you translate the concept of "observing" Jesus in action? How can we do this today?

_____

_____

_____

_____

_____

_____

_____

_____

_____

_____

Take a moment to comment on what it means to "follow" Jesus today.

Since we cannot follow Jesus physically around today, how do we follow him in a metaphysical or spiritual sense?

_____

_____

_____

_____

_____

_____

_____

_____

_____

We noted that true disciples "understood" Jesus' teaching and mission. What specifically are you doing to understand Jesus' teaching?

_____

_____

_____

_____

_____

Take some space and write down some ways that you can accomplish the commission of Jesus to his disciples in Mt 28:19ff. How can you personally carry out Jesus' command to reach the nations by making disciples?

_____

_____

_____

_____

_____

_____

_____

_____

_____

_____

BIBLIOGRAPHY

Blomberg, Craig L. "Matthew" *Commentary on the New Testament Use of the Old*. Gen Ed. G.K. Beale and D.A. Carson. Grand Rapids: Baker Academic, 2007.

Byrskog, Samuel. *Jesus the Only Teacher: Didactic Authority and Transmission in Ancient Israel, Ancient Judaism, and the Matthean Community*. Almqvist & Wiksell International: Stockholm, 1994.

Carson, D.A. "Matthew." in *The Expositors Bible Commentary*. F.E. Gaebelein (ed.). vol. 8. Grand Rapids: Zondervan, 1984.

Evans, Craig. "Matthew – Luke." in *The Bible Knowledge Background Commentary*. Colorado Springs: David C. Cook Publishers, 2005.

Fee, Gordon. *God's Empowering Presence*. Peabody Massachusetts: Hendrickson Publishers, 1992.

France, R.T. *The Gospel of Matthew*. in The New International Commentary of the NT. Grand Rapids: Eerdmans, 2007.

Keener, Craig. *A Commentary on the Gospel of Matthew*. Grand Rapids: Eerdmans, 1999.

_____. *The Gospel of Matthew: A Socio-Rhetorical Commentary*. Grand Rapids: Eerdmans, 2009.

_____. *The IVP Bible Background Commentary: New Testament*. Downers Grove: Intervarsity Press, 1993.

Nolland, John. "The Gospel of Matthew: a Commentary on the Greek Text", in *The New International Greek Testament Commentary*. Grand Rapids: Wm. B. Eerdmans Publishing, 2005.

Ogden, Greg. *Transforming Discipleship*. Downers Grove: IVP, 2003.

Wallace, Daniel B. *Matthew: Introduction, Argument, and Outline*. Dallas: Biblical Studies Press, 1997.

Wilkins, Michael. *Discipleship in the Ancient World and Matthew's Gospel*. Baker Books: Grand Rapids, 1992.

_____. *Following the Master: A Biblical Theology of Discipleship*. Grand Rapids: Zondervan, 1992.

_____. *In His Image: Reflecting Christ in Everyday Life*. Colorado Springs: NavPress, 1997.

_____. "Matthew" in *The NIV Application Commentary*. Grand Rapids: Zondervan, 2004. 21.

Willard, Dallas. *Renovation of the Heart: Putting on the Character of Christ*. Colorado Springs: NavPress, 2002.

Witherington, Ben III. "Matthew," in *Smyth and Helwys Biblical Commentary*. vol. 19. Macon: Smyth & Helwys Publishing, 2006.

Wright, N.T. *Jesus and the Victory of God: Christian Origins and the Question of God*. vol. 2. Minneapolis: Fortress Press, 1996.

_____. *The New Testament and the People of God*. vol. 1. Minneapolis: Fortress Press, 1996.

Young, Brad. *Meet the Rabbis*. Peabody: Hendrickson Publishers, 2007.

Made in the USA
Monee, IL
30 September 2019